POTTY TRAINING IN 5 DAYS

*The Complete Guide to Potty Training,
A Step-by-Step Plan for a Clean Break from
Dirty Diaper.*

Daniel Rott

Contents

Why Potty Training Your Child is Important

Making your child learn about potty training is indeed a new milestone that will help your child get accustomed to the everyday routine. Toilet training helps your child in controlling her urine as well as the body's bowel movements.

Therefore, accidents and difficulties are bound to get in your way. Punishments should not be used during potty training. You have to make sure that your child forms an understanding with your thoughts and expectations, which will prove to a successful recipe during this period.

Reasons Why It Is Important To Train Your Child for Potty

- The Social Reason

No matter where you live, society will always dictate the way you lead your daily life. And the same will be applied to your child as well. Beyond early childhood, it is not acceptable to see a child using diapers for potty purposes. Therefore, the right kind of attitude is required in this case, so that you don't offend your peers. The social pressure can also come from parents of other children as well.

Of course, the social pressure will also depend on the culture where you live, but as a rule of thumb, in most cultures, potty training starts at babyhood. Moreover, within a year or two of the child's age, it will be considered unacceptable to wear diapers. In the USA, diapers are considered unacceptable after the child is four years of age.

- The Self Confidence Reason

It has been reported that children who are potty trained in their babyhood days show a sense of self-confidence when compared to the children who are not. This type of self-confidence will give the child a better positive self-image at school. She will also feel confident among her friends because it will be a sense of accomplishment for her. It will also make the child happy and confident that she has control over her body.

- The Health Reason

It should not come as a surprise that potty training has a range of health advantages. The first health reason is the child's ability to control her bowel movements. This will indeed help in lowering the risk for any kind of bowel or urinary problems.

The children who are potty trained experience very fewer diseases that are fecal-related, which includes diarrhea and constipation. It will also help the child avoid any kind of fecal inconsistency too. The cleanliness is very important especially if the child is going to a pre-school or a day-care, as it can affect other children as well.

- The Environmental Reason

This reason is mostly avoided by most parents and can be an afterthought because being potty trained is the greener way to live. Disposable diapers are indeed very hard to recycle and also contribute to landfills. These diapers never decompose and even block drains and sewers, and also may end up in the stomach of domestic animals like stray cows and buffaloes.

Recycling these diapers require energy and resources, and therefore if your child is potty trained, then you'll be saving the environment' resources, energy and will also be doing your bit in controlling diaper garbage as well.

When Is the Right Time to Do It?

In the previous section, we had already talked about the importance of potty training and also all its advantages. However, how should you know that your child is ready to be potty trained, right?

There are various specific signs that you should look into your child to make sure that he or she is mature enough to learn this task. It has been researched and therefore, has been found out that girls tend to show more interest in getting potty trained than boys. In fact, girls show signs of being ready to be potty trained almost two or three months before than boys.

Even though there is no specific right time to do it, we will discuss the consensus that will help you know that your child is ready to be potty trained.

- Most healthy children do not have the emotional and physical well-being to start getting potty trained before 18 months of age, which can also extend up to three years as well. It should be kept in mind that the right time for boys will always be a few months later than girls.
- Parents plan to potty train their kids between two to three years of age, as it gives the child a lot more extra time to get matured.
- Since there is no official age for getting potty trained, you should not hurry up the process for your child. If you don't want to train your child at an infancy age, then you should not -- at all costs. This is because a process like this needs the other person to fully understand your instructions. And if your child is still not receptive to your instructions, it's always better to not force him or her. Make sure that your child gains enough interest in learning this procedure. This is because, if the child is a school or a day-care goer, then she may face stressful occasions because the toilet set up might be different than what she is accustomed at home. Many parents make this

mistake of making their child learn about potty training too early for their age.

- Children under the age of two years might not have enough control over her body, especially over the muscles that control their rectum for potty, which may lead to accidents. Therefore, waiting until your child is at least 18 months to two years of age will be the best policy.

- Potty training is not only about just releasing the fecal matter in the toilet but also knowing how to flush the toilet, how to pull up the clothes during the procedure and also learn to wipe bottom without the parents' help. A lot of these actions take time to learn and therefore most children do not develop these habits until they are at least three to four years old. Thus, you have to plan accordingly.

How to Know If Your Child Is Ready

By this time, it is a surety that you have got a rough knowledge of when to let your child start the strenuous procedure for potty training. Still, we feel that this rough knowledge is not enough, and as a parent, you must know about the various signs that will tell you clearly that your child is ready to be potty trained.

Before we start listing out the various signs, as a parent, you should always follow the footsteps of the child and go at her pace. You should always be praiseworthy and positive towards your child. Motivation is also key to keep your child consistent and interested.

Signs That Tell You That Your Child Is Ready To Be Potty Trained

- The Developmental Signs

Developmental signs will make the entire procedure much easier and effective. The first sign would be the ability of the child to show her independence. Having the desire is the ultimate key to learning to use the toilet for potty.

As a parent, you can also instill interest in your child by showing videos or reading books as well. Doing so, you'll be able to make your child more mature. It will also help the child in knowing her bowel movements because this will, in turn, give rise to facial expressions that the child can use to let you know that she needs to use the toilet. The more you encourage this kind of behavior with love and happiness, the more confident your child will grow.

- The External Signs

If your child has gained the capability to stay dry for at least two hours or more, then it is a clear sign that the child is ready to be potty trained. This is because the child has earned the sense of having a bowel movement that is regular and also can be predictable as well. This capability will also allow her to control the muscles around the rectum.

It is also the sign that the child's urinary bladder has increased in capacity and can hold urine for a much longer time than before.

- The Movement Signs

In order to be sufficiently potty trained, your child needs to be able to walk and run well. Movement is one of the most important factors which will allow the child to reach the toilet in just the right time in order to defecate or urinate. Also, sitting in the right way inside the toilet is also required for sufficient muscle contraction and relaxation during urination or defecation.

You can tell a child is ready by seeing that she is taking instructions from you and also following what you are saying. This will help the child to imitate all the actions that you teach her in the toilet, like cleaning her bottom after defecating, flushing the toilet, washing the hands with soap and water, using the rolled toilet paper in the right way, etcetera.

The child will also be able to learn to pull their clothes up or down (undress) which will clearly let you know that he or she needs to go to the toilet.

- Reporting or Behavioral Signs

Most parents use diapers for their children for up to two years of age of the child. Therefore, during that time, if you see your child getting the sensible feeling that she is able to report about a soiled diaper and thereby wants a clean one, you will definitely be sure that the child is ready to be potty trained.

In case your child has learned to say a few words, and she can pronounce the word *'toilet'* in any form or manner, this is the time to ensure that the child is ready to get potty trained.

Things to Keep In Mind When Potty Training Your Child

- Always try to encourage your child and do not scold her for any kind of toilet-related accidents. It can negatively affect the child, which will make her shy and hideous.
- Plan to co-operate with your child during this procedure as she needs all the support from her parents. Scolding or making negative comments during the process is not at all recommended.
- Forcing your child or giving punishment is not the right way to do it. The training process should always be made fun and enjoyable for your child. You can recite stories and poems during the process to make it less stressful.
- Do not let any external negative pressure get into the mind of your child. Your job, as a parent, should be to ease off the child's anxiety and keep the views of your family at bay.

Risks of Potty Training Your Child at a Later Stage (Mostly After Four Years)

- The child may develop the risk of various infectious diseases, like diarrhea.
- Bladder and rectum muscles of the child may function poorly, and therefore, they can be the cause for any kind of abnormal urination.
- There can be accidents during day-time or even during night-time sleeping.
- The child will not be able to control her potty habits, and therefore, a normal routine cannot be maintained.
- The onset of fear of going to the toilet may haunt the child since she is still not fully accustomed to the process. This can lead to serious loss of self-confidence and motivation. In worse case scenarios, the child may even suffer from constipation and therefore refuse to visit the toilet.
- Since the child will be using diapers for an extended period of

time, skin infections, reduction in the body's immunity, eye irritation, and the like, are some of the most dangerous issues that she can face.

- Finally, the child may develop any urinary tract infections or even other related health problems as well.

The Time It Can Take For Potty Training

It shouldn't come as a surprise that potty training is one of the most important childhood development milestones for your kid. Therefore, the process can turn out to be both challenging as well as commissioning both for the parent as well as the child. There will also be several other developmental events in your child's life, be it her ability to talk or even walk, but potty training is such an event that totally depends upon the respective parent to initiate.

As a parent, you definitely must be unsure about the time it will take your child to potty train, and that is the reason why we will discuss this aspect here to let you know about the rough estimation of the time it will take for such an event.

Of course, there is no such single right answer to that question, since every kid is different, it is still possible to make that prediction or suggestion.

- The Dependence on the Method

The time for your child will very much depend on the kind of training technique you'll be using. Some parents try to train their child with the help of 7-day plans, while others use the potty training procedure over a certain number of months.

There have been many children who had been successful with the help of a 5-day potty training plan. During these five days, the parents always provide undivided attention towards their children by stopping the immediate use of diapers and thereby increasing the amount of fluid intake.

When parents cannot dedicate a special amount of time to their children that is when potty training across a period of several months will seem like a no-brainer. Techniques like the Elimination Communication Method uses six months in order to train your child for potty. Therefore, the time factor will depend on what move you choose and also the compatibility of that move with your child.

It has already been reported by the University of Michigan Medicine that it is very common for children to wet their bed up to the age of five years. As a parent, you should not worry much, since your child will be able to control her urinary bladder as well as her bowel movements within 3 - 4 years of age.

- The Dependence on the Age

Most kids will show signs of potty training readiness within 24 months or simply two years. So, if you start earlier than what it is intended for your child, it may take longer, since the child will not have enough maturity to take it all in.

There are also various other medical conditions which can arise if you start the process early, including the risk of urinary tract infections due to the child holding the urine for extended periods of time, wetting of the bed, constipation and other relevant accidents.

The American Academy of Pediatrics had reported that as a parent, if you wait out a bit longer than the usual 24 months, then your child will be much quicker in grasping the process since she will have the necessary skills in order to be self-confident and self-sufficient. On the other hand, if you wait for too long, then it can be a future problem when attending daycare school, and this might interrupt your child's playing time.

It will not be in the best interest of your child to put the pressure of a specific timeline on her head, in order to finish the potty training. The average timeline is there for a reason, and that is to give you an idea. Your child can complete the process sooner or later than what the normal timeline is, and it should be accepted regardless.

The potty training procedure is a marvelous experience-worth journey for every child and her parent(s). So, researching about the various training methods and then finally selecting the most appropriate one for your child's special requirements should be your job.

There is no exact way to tell the time, except that is will be proportional to the age and the training method you choose for your child. You can always get help from your pediatrician, in case you're concerned about your child's development or need any other assistance, in regards to the potty training.

Busting Some Myths about Potty Training

Myths are indeed very funny things, and busting them is even funnier. A lie if repeated several times can become the truth, and that is the exact case with myths. Myths are nothing but a simple repetition of words that you hear again and again, and therefore, it makes you think that the words are indeed the truth. There are also other times when you think that something is true and thus, you support anyone who believes the same as well.

When it comes to potty training, several myths had been passed down by our family members and the community. Moreover, the worst thing is that we believe in them. Therefore, it is time to bust some of the most common potty training myths that have been floating among parents for a very long time indeed.

- Myth #1: Potty Training Should Start Within 24 Months

False. A child's potty training depends upon several different aspects, which include both physical and mental development. Therefore, unless you get the signs of readiness from your child, then there is no use to initiate the procedure. The signs of readiness can come at any age, and therefore, you have to know when your child is ready.

Nature doesn't always go according to the plan, and the same can be said for your child. You have to wait for your child to become mature enough to endure this challenging situation.

- Myth #2: The Child Will Be Potty Training Ready All By Herself

False. Your child, who hasn't yet matured fully will not be able to express her feelings in the right way. Therefore, relying on her to let you know that she's ready will be a foolish job. You cannot tell a child is ready if she shows interest or curiosity in the toilet. Thus, you have to know that all by yourself, as a parent.

Build your child's interest appropriately. Your child will start to look at the toilet training as an important activity, and that is how you can create the opportunity to make your child learn about the method. This will also help in making your child learn about the other toilet etiquettes, like flushing the toilet after excreting, washing hands and bottom thoroughly with soap and water, and the like.

- Myth #3: Training Will Be Done In a Matter of Days

False. While some parents might have found their success through the various 'days' method, the situation might not be the same for your child. The truth is that most children will take the longer route before eventually learning how to do potty or urination in the right way. The time can range from just mere weeks to even months.

There are also several cases where parents had to stop their training half-way through because it was not going according to their plan and therefore, had to start over at a later date and finally find success. Your children can also regress after learning the training too, as small accidents might continue to happen later onwards due to life changes. They might also start attending a day-care school, which might make things tough.

- Myth #4: Boys Are Always Difficult To Train than Girls

False. Not 'always.'

It is not about gender, but it is about the uniqueness that defines your particular child. Some boys like to drink milk more than girls - but that doesn't mean that boys, in general, like to drink milk more than girls. Generalization should not happen.

Every child is different and therefore, sometimes even girls can also be harder to train than boys. It all depends upon your approach and your own method. Easy is a relative term that should be taken with a huge grain of salt.

Yes, there might be small differences, as in days or months, but not in years. Small boys and girls should be considered similar than different.

- Myth #5: Night-time Potty Training is Not Necessary

False. Night-time potty training procedure is just as important as doing the daytime training. Many parents think that if the child does her potty training in the right way during the daytime, then night-time will not be an issue.

But the truth is that children can still have accidents at night, especially when the child is in a sleepy mood and does not have the psychological backing of the parent, as during the daytime.

You have to train your child in the same manner as you'd do in the daytime. Otherwise, bed-wetting can be a serious problem at a later date.

- Myth #6: Using Rewards Are the Easiest Way to Learn Potty Training

False. At the beginning of the process, it might seem evident that you'll need the help of your child's favorite treats in order to make her interested in this training exercise. However, once you see your child is getting the hang of things, it is not recommended to continue the process.

Instead, using practices like appreciating or encouraging children by hugging or doing high-fives will be the best way to mitigate this issue.

As a parent, you don't want your child to get spoiled by treats. Nor you would want to hand over a treat to your child every time she uses the toilet. It will just be impractical and irresponsible.

- Myth #7: Potty Training Should Not Be Done In Winter

False. It is not recommended that you just hold off your child's potty training exercise just because it is winter outside and the temperature is low. This should not be an excuse at all.

Potty training exercise can be done at any time or season during the year, just when you know that your child is ready to take in the learning experience. The process might not be what you had hoped for, because of the cold, but that is fine and the training will be well worth the pain.

Myths are certain beliefs that hold us back and do not let us think outside of the box by any means. When it comes to potty training, you have to be really flexible in your approach and adapt to the likes and dislikes of your child. You have to keep an open mind, know all the strengths and weaknesses of your child, and then move forward. Hopefully, these seven myth-busters will aid you in your journey.

Potty Training Essentials to Know

Is your child ready? Decided to finally make your child learn about the potty training exercise? Then you need to know about essential things before you start. These essentials contain are some of the most important products that you need to shop in order to make the process a lot easier and successful.

The training procedure is certainly not intricate as you might think it is, but it sure does require some of the best efforts from your side along with time and patience. These essential products can be easily obtained at any nearby children's store or super-market, so you don't have to worry much.

Essentials That You Should Keep Beside You

- Toilet Potty Seat and a Stepping Stool

This is one of the first essential items that you should buy before you start the training. The seat can be attached to the actual toilet, and it will provide the comfortable curves and grooves to let your child seat easily.

The reason is that when your child is first starting, she will need to figure out the posture and also get the rough idea about what it is like to sit on the toilet seat. It will help in building the excitement too. You also have to keep the toilet seat cleaned every day so that it can smell nice and not turn out to be unhealthy for your kid.

The stepping stool will help your child reach the sink to wash her hands or even grab the towel from the hanger. Do keep the soap and towels in a place where your child can reach easily.

- Pants with a Simple Waistband

During the potty training exercise, you can either keep your child naked or in underwear or keep her wearing a simple pant with a waistband around it. This will help in keeping the matters simple so that when the pressure builds up, your kid can go to the toilet with ease by just pulling down the pants.

Pants with buttons and zippers can be a real nightmare to deal with for your child, especially at the time when she needs to urinate or defecate.

- Chocolates and Sweets

You should keep your child's favorite treats handy beforehand because treats are what your child will need in stay motivated and encouraged. During the training exercise, you can decide to provide treats to your child for every right action, which will create a positive impact on her self-confidence. Make sure that you don't go overboard with your treats and rewards, as it may spoil the natural side of your child.

- Lots of Underwear

At the beginning of the potty training exercise, you might have to deal with several accidents. Therefore, you have to make sure that you keep a clean wardrobe ready for her, so that you can keep changing her toilet-soiled underwear since you'll not be using diapers.

Having a bunch of new and clean underwear at your home means that you don't have to worry about cleaning the soiled ones again and again. A simple laundry at the end of the day or the start of the next day should be enough. This will eliminate some of the unnecessary hassles.

- Training Exercise Chart

While this essential is not mandatory, keeping it will be a nice touch for tracking the progress of your child throughout the potty training procedure. You can buy a long nice chart paper and make your own custom plan, or you can buy a wall-hanging calendar as well.

You can keep it in the toilet or hang it just outside the toilet door. This will act as a reminder for both your child and yourself.

- Children's Books

Children love good stories and poems. Therefore, buying some children's story and/or poem books will be the best idea, as you can recite them to your kid during the potty time. It will help in clearing your child's mind and take her consciousness off to something else. She'll love when you recite her favorite childish stories happily and cheerfully. This will also boost the parent-child relationship.

- Disinfectant Disposable Wipes

There will be accidents during your child's training and in order to clean any kind of spills, you'll need cleaning wipes to take the spills off your carpet, or furniture, or even the ceramic or wooden floor. These wipes are very easy to use and will help your house smell a lot better. It will also keep the bacteria and germs at bay.

- Mattress Cover That Is Waterproof or Water-resistant

Since you'll not only have to train your child during daytime but night-time as well, bed-wetting can be a serious problem, if you don't take good measures beforehand. You have to ensure that when your child sleeps on the bed, there is enough protection so that the bed doesn't get soiled with potty or urine.

You can easily shop for a mattress cover at your local bedding store or super-market with in-built zippers for ease of use.

Common Potty Training Problems

Success and difficulties are what defines the whole procedure of the potty training exercise. We, as humans, are prone to errors and therefore, there will be times when your child will develop a fear of uncertainty during any stage of the plan, be it at the beginning or even months later.

Your child can face various issues while getting potty trained. Thus, you need to know the diverse solutions that you can get for those problems as well. Here, we will discuss some of the common problems that your child can face during potty training and how you can help to sort them out.

Potty Training Problems That You Should Be Aware Of

- The Fear Of The Toilet

It can seem a bit weird but to a small child, the idea of using a toilet can be pretty intimidating. From sitting in the toilet to flushing the toilet, everything about the toilet can easily alienate a child. The fear mostly comes from a past bad experience or it can come from prejudice as well.

The best way to tackle this issue is to train your child and allow your child to act under your supervision.

- Regression In The Usual Routine

Regression is pretty easy to experience for your child in environments that are unfamiliar to her. Any change in everyday liveliness would result in your child getting a simple setback, which can definitely lead to accidents and mishaps. The easiest and safest temporary solution would be to use diapers for the time being. Make the transition to the normal routine once your child feels comfortable.

- Not Going To The Toilet In The Right Time

Sometimes, if your child is too busy doing something else like playing or drawing, the chances are that she'll forget about the urge of going to the toilet at the right time and then when it'll be too late, accidents will happen. In order to mitigate this issue, you have to keep reminding your child about the toilet. It will help your child to start understanding the situation and eventually learn.

- Unsatisfactory Bowel Movements

The bowel movements of your child can be detected by just simply analyzing her stool. Large stools or small and hard stools are a clear indication that the bowel habit of your child is not right and she might be suffering from encopresis. It can affect your child just after the potty training exercise has been completed. You can change your child's bowel habits by feeding her more nutritious food products at regular intervals because, during the potty training exercise, your child was subjected to excessive fluids and treats, which are not good for the bowel movements.

- Concealing And Withholding Potty

Unsatisfactory bowel movements can make your child withhold potty or urine. They might also be developing the tendency to hide until the urge to go to the toilet goes away. This can be due to shame or fear as well. Withholding of potty can lead to hardening of the stool, which in turn, can turn out to be painful later on for your child.

You have to use numerous pictures, stories and also play games with your child in order to encourage your child to go to the toilet and thereby overcome the fear.

Potty Training Tips for Boys

Scientific research has shown that the brain of a boy develops very differently than a girl. You have to perform certain things differently while potty training boys when compared to girls. Boys are a lot more interested in playing outside or indoors. Therefore, getting them to learn about something such as potty training can indeed be challenging.

You have to keep these following best tips in mind when potty training your small boy.

Training Tips for Boys to Keep In Mind as a Parent

- Make Sure To Not Rush The Process

The popular notion that girls are easy to potty train when compared to boys can really get into your head and therefore the whole process can turn out to be a disaster. Keep in mind. It is natural for any human being, especially your child, to take his own time in learning the process. The potty training procedure is one of the most important habits that your boy will possess and rushing it will be the worst thing you can do.

- Train With His Friend, Father Or His Older Sibling

There's no better way to teach your small boy about potty training than to let him copy his own brother or father. The child will understand the process naturally because of how human beings are created into two different sexes.

You can also train your small boy with a friend of his if you happen to know the boy's parents. This will make exercise enjoyable for everyone. Furthermore, your small boy will be very much inspired by his friend's progress and therefore, will be more encouraged to continue, because eventually, the competition factor will kick in.

- Let Your Boy Learn About When To Stand Up And Sit Down

Making your boy to learn the differences between when to stand up and when to sit down can be time-consuming. You have to let him practice in separate postures, but before you do that, you have to first start by letting your boy sit down for both potty and urination. After some time, you can allow the transition to standing up during urination.

- Time To Practice Targets

Since girls do not have to practice targets while urinating, there is less work involved. But, with boys, you have to make him practice how to urinate in the right way, inside the toilet, so that you don't end up with a messed up toilet room.

After your small boy starts to understand the differences between sitting down and standing up, you can let him learn about targeting his urine in the right manner, so that it ends up inside the toilet.

- Always Be Loving And Encouraging

Doesn't matter if it's a boy or a girl, every child needs love and care. It will help in bringing out the best in your small boy. The time when he'll learn that as a parent, you are always motivating and praising him - his self-esteem and confidence will increase multi-folds and it will surely aid in the success of this training plan.

Potty Training Tips for Girls

Even though the potty training procedure is followed in the same way for both boys and girls, there are still some minor differences that as a parent of a daughter should keep in mind. There is a popular notion among numerous parents that girls tend to finish their training a lot earlier than boys - which is kind of debatable since it depends on that particular child.

Regardless of what you might think - in case your small little daughter is ready to be potty trained, it is time that you should follow the below mentioned training tips that will help your child to have a better understanding of the situation and will provide visible results.

Training Tips for Girls to Keep In Mind as a Parent

- Ask Your Daughter's Feelings And Make Sure She's Ready

There is no better way to start the training procedure after knowing that your child is happy about it and is ready to learn as well. If she is not ready, then do not coerce her into this training plan. You have to talk to your daughter personally and ask her about she feels about getting to know about these new habits. If she's excited and not too bothered with the failures, then you can start off.

- Let Your Daughter Know About The Toilet And Also Learn From You

When your daughter will see the toilet all by herself and will know how her dad and mom use it, then it will easier for her to learn the whole thing. You can demonstrate her how the toilet functions and also to use it in the right way. You have to also let her know to wash her hands and be hygienic, in order to keep the germs at bay.

- Make The Process Fun

It will be better for your child if you can only focus on the positives and keep the process fun and exciting. You have to keep the motivation, encouragement and the praises high. Refrain from being over-enthusiastic, because it may kill the flow. Instead, remain patient and calm and help your daughter to relax and continue the training.

- Chalk Out A Routine And Be Clear In Your Teaching

A daily routine is necessary for a potty training exercise. As a parent, you need to know the times when your child requires to go to the toilet so that even if you forget reminding your daughter, she will still remember.

Apart from that, you have to be straight-cut in your teaching methods, so that your child understands your words right away and do not misinterpret.

- Use Comfortable Clothes For Your Daughter And Ensure That She Wipes Correctly

Make her wear easy and comfortable clothes are recommended so that she can easily undress. Also, you should ensure that your daughter wipes in the right way, otherwise there will be a risk of urinary tract infections. Wiping from front to the backside is recommended and it should be followed by your daughter at all times.

Preparing Your Child for the Potty Training

Most toddlers can be potty trained when they are two to three years of age. Even though some children might show early signs, 24 months is the sweet spot to prepare your child for potty training. Therefore, in order to make sure that you train your child in the best possible manner, you have to first know the various tidbits about the process.

Good preparation is the key to success. Pre-potty training preparation is important because you will be making your child comfortable and ready for the upcoming situation. The following are some of the most crucial suggestions that should be taken into account.

Suggestions for Preparing Your Child

1. Making Your Child Learn About The Word 'Potty'

Two and three-year-olds hardly know how to vocalize words, apart from the occasional 'Mam' and 'Dad' pronunciations. Therefore, it is your duty to make sure that your child not only learns about the 'potty' word but also know how to speak it as well.

Speaking is very important in this case besides knowing, because your child will be able to let you know when she would like to go to the toilet. It will be a direct way of communicating with your child. Over time, your child will start to know the meaning of the word and it will become easier for you to ease the training procedure.

2. Introducing The Toilet To Your Child

First, you have to get her interested in the matter and for that reason, you need to make sure that you talk and read about the toilet with your kid. You can even let your child watch when you use the toilet.

You have to show your child how to lift off the toilet cover or lid, or how to flush the toilet, and so on.

Seeing is believing and if you familiarize your child with the toilet, then she will not be scared of using it. This will help her in learning much faster and in a more natural manner.

3. Setting Up The Stage For The 5-Day Plan Beforehand

The actual potty training can be frustrating if you don't know about the tips and tricks. Many parents start without researching and then get frustrated half-way. Make sure you read about the entire 5-day potty training guide so that you can get to know the dos and don'ts of the method.

It is not recommended that you stick to a certain strict procedure. Instead, be adaptive and flexible so that your child can learn in the way that she'd like. Make changes to the training system, whenever you feel that there is a need. Every child is different and thus what works for one child might not work for the other. You should, at all times, stop comparing your child to the others and let your child go through the process on her own caliber.

Potty Training Plan for Your Kid

As your child starts to grow and becomes more mature, potty training is one of the essential habits that you'd want your kid to possess. Wrestling with diapers throughout the day is the worst thing that you want to do, and therefore you must take the initiative of making your child learn about the process.

The thing which should be taken care of is that you ease your child throughout the whole process. This is the reason why a five-day plan is much better than other shorter spanned plans like two-days or even three-days as well.

Devotion and motivation are highly required between these days, both from your part and your child as well. In this article guide, we will go through all the essentials that you'll require in order to make your child be potty trained within five days.

Things to Keep in Mind before You Start

- Since this procedure requires training your child on how to use the toilet by herself, the first thing to do is to set aside all your child's diapers for the next five days. Also, you need to make sure that you're always beside your child at home, so that you can supervise the whole method.
- Secondly, you should keep yourself free. Your child will need your support and therefore you really do not want to get busy with something that will hamper the training. Make sure you keep your child in t-shirt and underwear, with no such use of diapers or even baby pants. This will help your child to think and react accordingly when she has a potty accident.
- Finally, you should allow your child to have as much food and liquids as she likes. Without eating more than usual, the

pressure for potty or even urination will not build. Therefore, you should shop for your child's favorite snacks beforehand. Going overboard with junk foods is not recommended.

With those elements out of the way, let's get down into the more exciting part.

Day 1

The first day is the most crucial one. You have to make sure that your kid understands what you want her to do. The better way to make this happen is to explain the whole scenario to your child. Children love treats and snacks, so letting your child have a treat every time she does the right thing will boost the self-confidence.

Don't make your child wear diapers on the first day. Instead, use underwear or you can keep your child naked with an oversized t-shirt that will cover her private parts. This is because the less obstruction there is between your child's bottom and the potty, the better it will be for your kid.

In case the temperature is cold outside, you may want to increase the warmth of your room heater so that your child does not catch any cold. You can also use leg-warmers too, but make sure that there is no such obstructed access around the crotch.

During the first day, the main idea would be to allow your child to try to excrete a lot more than usual. This will help your child to get as much practice as possible within a short period of time. This is why making your child drink snacks and fluids throughout the day is very necessary.

Letting your child drink much juice, mainly fruit juice, will be the best idea since it will not only be healthy for her, but it will also build the pressure of urinating as well. But, don't provide your child with excessive juice. Otherwise, it may lead to diarrhea. Mixing juice with a little bit of water is a good idea.

Make sure your child follows your instructions and goes to the toilet just when she feels the pressure of potty. There will be some minor or major accidents due to timing issues, but the best thing would be to ensure that she tries to put your instructions into actions.

Also, provide your child with treats every time she follows your guidance. Don't forget to change the clothes, if required. This will mark the end of the first day, and now it's time to continue this training the next day.

Day 2

The second day will a straight-up continuation of the previous day. This means that your job will be to closely follow her throughout the day and night and make sure that she does not forget about your instructions of the previous day and continues to follow them the rest of the day. If your child encounters any mistake, it will be your duty to rectify them.

Your child may be reluctant to use the toilet starting the second day, but you must encourage her. This will make your child gain self-awareness and you will see glimpses of progress via this method. Continue with the glorious treats that you were previously giving her.

 Treats like gummy bears or sweet tarts would be a nice idea. In case you feel that your child is not getting enough potty or urination pressure, then you can also resort back to the use of fluids again. However, make sure that you feed in a limit.

As a parent, you might ask that the use of treats and juices can be injurious to the health of the child. Well, treats will only be used for the first training procedure, and over time, you should start to phase out the treats and juices and let your kid use the toilet like a normal human being. It will all be easy once you cross this hurdle.

Day 3

Day three will be the start of something extraordinary, and you will be able to see the fruits of your labor. Your child will start to use the toilet on her own, which will be a marvelous addition to your lifestyle.

The first thing you'd notice is that your child will start having the sense of going to the toilet just as when there will be a pressure for excreting. Thereby, there will be fewer accidents overall, and you will not have to clean up the mess again and again.

However, you would still need to be with your child at all times, to keep the accidents to the minimum. You have to be careful and alert at all times. From day three, it is advisable to reduce the intake of any kind of fluids, just for the training purposes because you need to bring down everything to the normal levels for your child.

However, you should not stop with the treats because it will be the only motivational cause for your child to continue during her training procedure.

Make sure that you always keep your child clean with nice underwear and t-shirt. Do not let your child wear pants at this stage because the process is still not yet completed, and there are again two more days left for your child to reciprocate as well.

The third day will also be significant for another reason, and that is your child's thought process. She will start to understand the underlying reason behind potty training. The appreciation will depend on your kid, but most of the times, you can be sure that your child will greatly appreciate your love and care towards him or her.

You also have to make sure that your child uses the toilet in the night time, just in the same way as in the morning. Accompanying her at night for urination or potty will help your child gain more courage to do things seamlessly.

Day 4

Accidents will no longer happen (or very less likely) from day four onwards. You will notice that your child will start to use the toilet without you needing to ask her, or even letting you know about it. Your child will embrace this training as the new habit, and therefore, it will come naturally.

Another thing that you will notice is that your child will need to change their clothes less often. At the end of the day, you don't have to worry about cleaning your child's soiled clothes. Apart from that, your child will also remain dry throughout the day.

From day four, you can decide whether you want to continue providing her with treats for the actions or not. You have to learn about the behavior and the psychology of your child in the right manner so that you can learn whether she will be happy without the treats or with them.

Talking with your child will be the best option as you'll start to know about the desires and the needs. In case your child wants you to continue giving treats, then definitely do so. You'd really don't want your child to get demotivated just as when the training is about to end.

The technique here will be to make sure that your child will return to her normal lifestyle. So, keep this thing in mind when providing her with treats.

Day 5

Depending on the situation of day four, day five will be the day when normalcy will be restored. You can easily notice this when you'll see your child taking off her clothes in order to go to the toilet for excretion. Even though this will be amazing for you as a parent, your work will not end here as you've also to make sure that she learns the toilet etiquettes as well.

The toilet etiquettes include flushing the toilet after excreting, lowering down the toilet cover, washing the hands and so on. Even though these things will take more time, day five will be the right time to learn about these etiquettes, so that your child can take care of everything and you don't have to interfere anymore.

Over time, things will improve, and your child will stop taking any more treats in order to go to the toilet. Your child will learn that potty like an old habit. They will feel comfortable on their own.

You can make them wear pants and other clothing types without fearing of any accidents. This trust will help your child make fewer mistakes in the future. Do not freak out even if accidents happen after day five, because it is a part of your process.

Extra Tips and Tricks

Let's face it. The hard part is really over, and you can now be free with the idea in mind that you have made your child learn a valuable lesson that will go with her lifelong. But, there are still small things that you should be making sure before calling it a day.

As a parent, you'll be needing these extra tips and tricks to make sure that you successfully complete the process.

- Train Your Child for Nighttime

While the 5-day training process does involve the inclusion of night-time training as well, you have to know that children take longest when it comes to potty training during night-time. Of course, your child can easily use the toilet during the day-time, but during the night, your child might find it difficult to control the urge to urinate.

Not every child will learn it at the same time. As a parent, you can use overnight training pants or even waterproof mattress covers until your child eventually learns about the process.

- Maintain Patience

It can be very annoying and boring to see your child in underwear and a t-shirt during this potty training procedure. Since you have to be with your child at all times, it can be nerve-wracking to manage other tasks, both on the personal and professional front.

But, you have to be patient and watch over your child's actions.

Make sure you keep your cool and not scare or punish your child for any type of accident. It is highly recommended to spend time with your child reading books and playing with toys during this 5-day training exercise. It will also be refreshing for you as you will get time to spend with your kid, away from the daily hectic schedule.

- Do Not Rely Much On Rewards

While we have already mentioned that giving treats for your actions is a nice gesture and it brings motivation to the table, over-reliance on rewards can be dangerous for the child's future aspects. You must provide your child with treats only during the training period.

Doctors say that praising your kid in the right manner every time will do more good, than handing over a bar of chocolate.

Therefore, you should learn and know the time when it is best to stop this practice. As we've suggested before in this guide, day five will be the right time to stop any rewards.

- Let Others Know of Your Child's Potty Training

In case your child is going to a daycare school or being taken care of by a caregiver or a nanny, then you should let them know of your child's situation. This is very important because you really don't want the caregiver to again resort to using diapers for your child.

It will be in the best interest for your child and the person taking care of. Ensure that the person is co-operative with your child, such that they may understand your child's situation properly and move ahead with the plan.

- Bring On Positivity

A positive attitude is very necessary to keep your child motivated during this 5-day potty training exercise. This is because children have their self-esteem, which should not be broken.

Even though you may want to make them do what you want by using anger or negative comments, but it will be just a fearful response from your child. Punishment can easily affect the relationship between the parent and child. You should not show any signs of frustration or displeasure to your child, as it can be a counter-productive step in the opposite direction.

- Make the Toilet Easily Accessible To Your Child

It can happen that sometimes you may forget about the training exercise and keep your toilet doors locked. Since children at this age cannot hold their potty or urination pressure for too long, it is always the best idea to keep your toilet door open at all times. You can buy a portable potty chair as well, in case of any emergencies. The faster it will be for your child to reach the toilet, the better it will be for your child's training exercise.

Sometimes, you may see that your child cannot hold the pressure and starts excreting in the middle of the room. During that time, it is your duty as a parent to show them the toilet entrance. The more you remind your child about the training procedure, the quicker she will learn.

- If There Are Emergencies At Home, Call Off the Training

Emergencies, in this case, mean someone at your house is sick or going through a rough period, maybe because of financial or personal issues. Your child cannot train in an environment that is hostile and not perfect. An environment like this will easily increase the tension and anxiety and therefore cannot be recommended since the last thing you want to do is to scream at your child for your own personal problems.

Always know the time when it is right to pull the plug and start over -- maybe after a week or a month later when everything is normal again.

After The 5-Day Plan

Five days can be a long time especially when things don't tend to go your way and you've to constantly make adjustments on the fly. But once you've completed the training with your child, it is the right time to make sure that your child is trained, and you don't have to revert to using diapers again.

Conclusion

There are truly many ways to potty train your child, but this five-day procedure seems the best in terms of pacing and also not overly intense as well. Some parents may take a shorter 2-days or 3-days process, but those processes will not help your child learn and practice in the best way possible.

Slow learning is very effective and therefore this method needs no further justification. It's simply a much better option for any simple child out there.

The biggest advantage that you'll take away from this procedure is that you and your child can start living diaper-free, which is very much worth all of this hassle. Make sure to buy lots of underwear for your child and stay positive with a bright smile. Use the evening and the night-time to recharge your energy, in order to navigate through these 5-days of excitement and learning experience for your little one.

Things to Look Out For After the Potty Training Plan Has Been Completed

1.   Always Keep The Enthusiasm And Celebration High

Enthusiasm and motivation are not only required to get you past the training phase but also to maintain enthusiasm during the learning phase. You have to ensure that your child follows the everyday routine of using the toilet. And for that, you need to keep your spirit of joy at an all-time high around your child.

Praises and high-fives will help in boosting self-confidence and determination in your kid.

2.   Potty Training When Sleeping And During Night-Time

Even though your child will learn about the potty training during the 5-day plan, you have to still allow your child to learn it fully, especially when she is sleeping and during night-time. Your child will need to know how to manage the pressure of urination or potty when she is in sleepy mode or even at 2 AM in the morning.

Night-time potty training will require more careful strategy and understanding, as you've to guide her to be more mature in handling her own matter.

3.   Take Care Of Accidents

If you think that the 5-day potty training plan will make your child a champion in using the toilet, then you're wrong. Accidents will continue to happen even after the procedure and you have to keep your patience and nerves so that you can point out the mistakes to your child.

It will take time before accidents will stop, but not immediately because children are slow learners and therefore you cannot force your child to learn such a complex training, very easily.

4.   Scope For Improvement

The training is not the end of the road for the entire learning experience. The training is just the beginning and it will act as a rightful path for your child to reach the final destination. But, before your child will reach the final destination, i.e. knowing all about using the toilet, you have to make sure that you stick by her side and correct every wrong. This is how you will be bringing up self-improvement in your kid.

Every parent would love their child to learn perfectly and with this attitude of correcting your child's mistakes every time, you will be able to make your kid the master of the potty training plan.

Potty Training Incentives That Work

Children are very hard to convince, but incentives make it easy. Incentives, in this case, are like the helping hands that will help you to reach your goal faster. There is no doubt that every child is unique in their own ways, but there are certain kinds of incentives that will cater to every kid out there.

Incentives will act as the pill of motivation for your youngsters in migrating from the old-age diapers to the new-age toilet. The following are some of the best potty incentives that you can use.

Incentives That Actually Help You to Accomplish the Potty Training Exercise

- Sweets and Treats

Kids love chocolates, gummy bears, jellies, and the like. Therefore, if you plan your potty training exercise with the use of treats for every successful visit to the toilet, then you have a very successful formula. Your kid will love going to the toilet for just getting a pack of her favorite treats.

- Story Books

Every child loves a fascinating fiction story, and that is why you need to stock up on special potty training books that you'll only recite to your child when she's in the toilet. Storybooks will make your child happy and will also ease off the tension of the on-going training exercise.

- Stickers and Charts

Your child would love to have a track record of her training method and the number of times she has visited the toilet. For this reason, you can keep a wall-hanging chart beside the toilet door and let your child use stickers every time she goes to the toilet. This will keep your kid to be engaged in this training exercise and will also provide you with a quick report on the step-by-step progress.

- Toys and Barbie Dolls

Toys are like the eternal spirit that every child loves to have, and therefore, they are indeed a nice incentive to encourage your kid with. The idea of toys will itself make any child go crazy and go to extreme lengths to even do the impossible. You have to take advantage of this and make your child learn in the best way possible, and if she succeeds, then rewarding her with her favorite toys will be heartwarming. If she doesn't succeed in the first step, you can always motivate her to do better next time.

- Lots of Praise

Connected with the previous incentive - you have to always shower your child with lots of praise and then even more. Children will always respond to simple motivational praises. Things like dancing or clapping are enough to make your child feel amazing and wonderful.

- Coloring Books

Simple coloring books with a set of pastel or marker colors will be perfect for getting your child interested. Children love to color and draw on their own because creativity will be at an all-time high when your child is young and energetic. The coloring book will act as her treasure or achievement for you to remember.

Frequently Asked Questions

What should I be doing if my child encounters a potty accident?

It should be kept in mind that accidents are a part of toilet training. Therefore, it is highly probable that your child will have sporadic accidents even after the potty training exercise is over and she learns to use the toilet. This is very normal and most children experience it as well.

There will be times when your child will get very much busy with her playing activities and will totally forget about needing to use the toilet. This is the reason why you need to remind your child at constant intervals about using the toilet. If you can recommend daily trips to your child, then it will help in preventing any kind of potty accidents.

In case, if your child does have an accident, then it is your duty to stay calm and handle the situation. You should not be punishing your child at all. You can easily change your child's clothes and then start encouraging her to use the toilet or the potty chair from next time. This will prevent your child from fearing the potty training procedure.

Should you be using training pants?

There have been various notions of using the training pant. There are doctors who are against the idea of using training pants. There are also parents who think that using training pants might confuse the child and therefore it will be better to use diapers instead. Using diapers can indeed slow down the potty training process lot since the training exercise itself recommends less usage of diapers.

Some parents are of the opinion that training pants are best suited to be used during the potty training exercise of your child. You can also use training pants during sleep-time or night-time when it is more difficult for the child to control her urge to urinate or potty.

Is the use of rewards recommended during the potty training exercise of my child?

The use of rewards will depend on how well your child responds to your action. There are kids who act well to rewards and incentives and therefore, you might use them it encouragement or motivation. These rewards range from using chocolate treats to using stickers, charts, and storybooks during bed-time.

There are numerous other parents who think that the potty training exercise should be done in a healthier manner and therefore, not using any kind of incentives should be the way to go. The best thing would be to ask your doctor about what are the advantages and disadvantages of using rewards and incentives so that you can decide the same on your own and then take the necessary decisions.

How should I know about the time that I should not try the toilet training exercise?

There will be several things which can come in your way of potty training. In case you or your child is going through a rough period of stress or change in the environment, then it is not the perfect time to start the potty training exercise.

Here are a few situations wherein you should avoid potty training your child:

- Avoid potty training if there is any change in the surrounding environment or you are planning to move to a different location. Changes in the environment affect the psychological behavior of your child.
- Your child has a new companion to play with and it can be a small brother or a sister, who has just born and has started

growing up in the same house.

- Your child may face difficulties if you've placed her in different childcare than what she was used to before.
- Children start their lives sitting and sleeping in a small crib. Therefore, when your child grows up and moves to the bed, the comfort factor will change and thus it can also affect the potty training procedure too.
- There might be a time when there are accidental deaths in your family. Your child can also suffer from any kind of significant disease, which can weaken her up. Other interruptions during normal life can also happen as well.
- In any case, if you've already planned and have been trying to potty train your child for many weeks and still she's not getting a hold of the experience, then it is suggested and that you stop the process for the time being. The main reason would be that your child is currently not yet ready to take in the potty training. As a caring parent, you should again revert to using diapers for the time being and then after a few months, you can proceed to try again.

What Questions Should You Ask The Doctor About Your Child?

- What should I be doing if my child is not coming on terms with me to sit on the potty?
- What to do if there is a power struggle between me and my child when I'm trying to make my child learn about the potty training exercise?
- What is the estimated amount of time that my child should take in order to be potty trained?
- My child is currently using diapers or training pants during sleeping and night-time. How long should I have to continue using diapers or training pants and how long should my child have to wear them as well?
- At first, my child had been following the potty training instructions in the right manner. But recently, she has started

making a lot of mistakes and therefore resulting in more accidents than ever before. What should be the problem in this case and what has exactly gone wrong in the training exercise?

- My child is currently four years old and it still not yet potty trained. What should I be doing?

All You Need To Know About Potty Training Guidelines

- It should be kept in mind that almost 98 percent of all children become daytime independent by four years of age.
- Each child is different, and therefore, the age to start potty training will also be different. The best age to start potty should be between 18 - 32 months of age. You can start your pre-potty training when your child is just ten months old.
- The potty training exercise can be started at any age, but the skills, biology, and readiness of your child will finally determine when she can take up toileting on her own.
- The way you should be teaching your child about the toilet should come naturally, just like teaching her the way to use a spoon or even building a block.
- It doesn't matter at what age your child starts the toilet training, because by two and a half years to four years of age, most of the children will become independently capable in using the toilet.
- It will generally take 12 months from the start of the training to full daytime toilet independence. The process will depend on how much skills of readiness your child will possess. The quicker it will be, the better.
- The future abilities or intelligence of a child, later on, doesn't depend upon the age in which she masters using the toilet.
- There is no single way to let your child learn about potty

training. If you are patient, pleasant and positive, any method can work for you.

- A child will only learn about night-time dryness when her physiology will support it. You cannot rush it.
- The readiness of the parent is just as important as the readiness of the child.
- The process of potty training is not supposed to be expensive. You'll just need a dozen of training pants, a potty chair, and a patient and a relaxed attitude as well.
- Most of the toddlers urinate at two-hour intervals, for about four to eight times a day.
- Every child has a regular bowel movement pattern. Some can have one or two, while others might have three times a day. Other children can even skip a day or two in between, as well.
- It has been found out that almost 80 percent of all children, during toilet training, experience setbacks. These setbacks are the key to mastering the process later on.

A quiz about Potty Training Readiness

It comes as no surprise that the potty training procedure will indeed happen faster if your child is ready in not only the physical aspects of things but also the social and cognitive aspects as well.

You may ask the question, how to know if your child is ready, right? In case, if you've never experienced this before, then you probably don't even know about the potty training readiness signs to look out for as well. You can, therefore, take the following quiz and thus decide on the readiness of your child.

- Situation #1

You can tell that your child is ready just by seeing her filing or wetting her diaper.

Choices:

1.   Never

2.   Sometimes

3.   Usually

- Situation #2

The number of times your child's diaper needs to be changed.

Choices:

1.   Often, every 2 hours

2.   The timing varies

3.   Every 2 - 3 hours and less often sometimes

- Situation #3

Your child knows the meaning of the words - sit, go, clean, dry, wet and wash.

Choices:

1.   No

2.   Few of them

3.   All of them

- Situation #4

When your child tries to communicate her needs, she usually,

Choices:

1.   Says a word or two or gives a sign and you guess the rest

2.   Mentions all the essential points

3.   Has the capability and the vocabulary to talk in sentences

- Situation #

 Giving your child a simple instruction, like putting something into a box, she,

Choices:

1.   Doesn't understand or follow the instructions

2.   Can perform the task if it coached to her or given a helping hand

3.   Can understand and does the job

- Situation #6

Your child can take off her pants and put them on again.

Choices:

1.   No

2.   Needs help

3.   Yes

- Situation #7

When you read a book to your child, she,

Choices:

1.   Ignores you

2.   Sometimes strays off and sometimes listens

3.   Will sit, listen and also enjoy the story as well

- Situation #8

Your child wants to do all things all by herself.

Choices:

1.   No

2.   Sometimes

3.   Every time

- Situation #9

According to you, is it the right time for potty training?

Choices:

1.   No

2.   Undecided

3.   Yes

Calculate the total number of responses for each numerical.

1. ____________

2. ____________

3. ____________

If most of your answers belong to the choice 1, then you should definitely wait and again test it out some months later.

In case, most of your answers belong to the choice 2, then it's time for the pre-potty training, and you have to get ready. Your child will not be suitable for live training, but pre-potty training will help your child to prepare for the future. You have to make a gradual introduction of various ideas and terms, which will make the overall training a lot easier.

Finally, if most of your answers belong to the choice 3, then your child is ready to be potty trained! The adventure is ready to be started and all the very best to you.

If you're stuck between two options or choices, then you have to put your own decision into the mix. No one will have a better knowledge of your kid than you do, and therefore, only you can direct your kid towards the perfect path.

All About Potty Training: Ready, Set, Go

Ready

You can already start the pre-potty training if your child has already celebrated her first birthday or even close to that date. These are very simple ideas that should lay down the groundwork for the potty training exercise and therefore, will make the process much easier and effective when you're going to start the plan.

- When you're changing your child's diapers, you have to describe the process to your child in order to teach her the words and also the meanings of various toilet-related purposes as well. These include words such as poo-poo and pee-pee. You also have to use descriptive words during processes such as dry, wet, wipe and wash.
- In case you're totally comfortable with the idea of bringing your child into the bathroom, you have to explain all the respective toilet etiquettes to her. You can let your child do the toilet flush and also make her know that as she'll grow up, she will have to use the toilet for poo-poo and pee-pee.
- You can start giving simple instructions to your child and help her to follow them as well. For example, you can ask your kid to put the spoon in the dishwasher or even bring her toy from the other room.
- You should be helping your child in identifying what is actually happening when she wets or fills her diaper. You can tell the respective words for the actions, such as pee-pee or poo-poo. Then you can let her watch you as you dump and flush the potty.
- The best way to help your child to learn about the training is to encourage her to do things all on her own. This includes allowing her to pull up her own pants, or fetching a book,

putting up on her socks or even carrying a cup to the sink as well.

- Take your time to sit daily with your child and have a storybook reading time together.
- You can always take the quiz for readiness after a few months to see the progress of our child and make sure if she's ready to take the potty training exercise.

Set

- You have to buy a potty chair along with some training pants, about four or more pants or shorts with an elasticated waist-band combined with a supply of pull-up disposable diapers and also a liner for feeling wetness sensation.
- You have put the potty chair in the toilet and then tell your kid about its functions.
- Make sure that you read books that are related to potty, to your child.
- Ensure that your child sits down on the potty chair and practice the action, without even expecting to do a pee-pee or a poo-poo.

Go

- It's time to start dressing up your child in pull-up diapers or even training pants.
- The best recommendation is to create a potty training plan or routine so that you can follow it every day. You can make a routine to allow your child to sit on the toilet in the morning after she wakes up, after taking meals, before going to bed or even getting inside the car or going out.
- In case your child says that she needs to use the toilet, don't ask any questions and just comply with your child's request.
- You should start the potty training by making your child sit down, be it a boy or a girl. For boys especially, standing and using the toilet can be practiced when he is tall enough to reach the toilet.

- Relaxing is the way to make your child go to the toilet. You can read a book to your child, tell her a story, sing with her or talk with her all day.
- Make sure that you make washing the hands a very important part of the routine, to maintain the hygiene. You have to keep a stool by the toilet sink, along with a hand-washing liquid or a soap. You can also buy colorful soaps specifically for your kid.
- Praising is a part of the process, and you always have to do it when she goes to the toilet.
- Always be patient and calm when cleaning up accidents made by your child.
- During night-time or bedtime, you can use diapers for our child.
- You can cover-up your car seats with a waterproof cover or start using pull-up diapers in your car as well.
- When you're away from home, ensure that you visit the new toilet with your child regularly. Children have a hard time when using the toilet in unfamiliar environments.
- Patience is the key. You have to wait for at least 12 months for your child to show independence in using the toilet.

Learn When To Stop

During the potty training procedure, if your child throws any kind of tantrums or even sheds her tears, or in case if you find yourself to be irritated or angry, then it is always a better choice to stop the training exercise. You have to review the training plan again and later on start the process all over.

You have to use a somewhat different approach in the second try, which can be held in the next month or two. But, for the first round, you can definitely follow this perfect article guide that we've laid down for you and your child.

Concluding the Potty Training

By now, you must have read all the essentials regarding the potty training program that we have put across. The whole process might overwhelm you a bit and therefore, it is crucial that you have a quick recapitulation guide so that you don't miss out on the necessary fundamentals.

This section will be all about the conclusive summary of the entire potty training exercise, which you can use to cross-check your progress throughout the whole operation.

Learning the Need to Potty Train

Before you start, as a parent, it will be wise to know the reasons which make the training compelling. There are several social, environmental and health reasons, apart from boosting the self-confidence of your own child, that you should understand.

Knowing the Right Time and If the Child is Ready

After you've known the important aspects of potty training, you have to make sure that your child is ready to be potty trained. Most children are trained for potty between the age of two and three years, which can also differ depending on the child's capability.

For this reason, you have to look at various signs that will tell you that your child is ready. Signs like your child is developing an interest when you mention about the toilet, can easily walk and move, has the capability to easily communicate with you, can carry out simple instructions, and the likes. Once your child is ready, you can start prepping for the training.

The Pre-Potty Training

The pre-potty training consists of all the required actions that you should try to impart to your child before the actual training commences. Actions like making your child know about the word 'potty' and also introducing your child to the toilet and its various etiquettes. You have to make sure that your child starts to follow your instructions, which will be important in making the training a success.

The pre-potty training will act as a second doorway to know if your child is active and sharp enough to undertake the procedure. As a parent, you also need to do your homework, learn about all the tips and tricks and perform your own research.

Shopping For the Potty Training Essentials

Before you start the potty training exercise, you have to shop for a number of products which will be needed during the course of the plan. You have to purchase lots of underwear, get your child's favorite treats and chocolates, purchase incentives or rewards for your child, stock up on a lot of disposable wipes, waterproof mattress covers, children storybooks, potty training chart and a host of other things.

The 5-Day Potty Training Plan

The potty training plan expands throughout five days and during these five days, you have to make your child learn about the exercise. The first day will be all about avoiding the diapers for your child and keeping a closer look on her, throughout the entire day.

Over the next couple of days, you have to make sure that your child becomes comfortable using the toilet and thereby, accidents will slowly start decreasing as well. You will notice that your child will be using the toilet on her own. During this time, having patience and remaining calm is the best thing you can do, since you have to constantly motivate and encourage your child to keep the spirits high.

Using various incentives is recommended during this phase, as it can help in boosting the morale of your child and get her more interested. Incentives like coloring books, storybooks, treats, chocolates, etcetera, should be more than enough.

Problems That You Can Face During or After the Potty Training Exercise

The process might not be smooth for every parent and there are some substantial problems that you may face during or after the training period. You child may experience fear of using the toilet or may suffer from bowel movement issues.

Any change in the environment or physical surroundings can also lead to regression in the toilet habits of your child. Your child may also withhold potty or urine over extended periods of time, which can lead to accidents. You have to ensure that you do not punish your child and instead try to adapt to the situation.

After The Potty Training Plan Has Been Completed

The completion of the training plan will not be the end of responsibilities for you, as a parent. After the training exercise, it is your duty to make sure that your child continues her current habits. You're expected to experience accidents, which you need to push aside and start aiming for improvements. Your enthusiasm should reflect on your child.

This is also the time when you should push for night-time potty training as well. Children are easy to train easily in the daytime, but you have to take special care for making them ready about night-time training exercise.

Separate Tips and Tricks for Girls and Boys

Even though the training procedure might be the same, there are some other things that you should keep in mind, when differentiating between a boy and a girl. Firstly, you have to make a boy learn when to sit down and when to stand up while using the toilet - which is not the case with a girl. Similarly, you have to allow a girl to learn to wipe in the right manner, which is from the front to the backside, in order to mitigate any urinary tract infections.

There are also other things that you should remember like, practicing your small boy using the toilet with his father or brother, which can easily aid in the continuation of the process or asking your small girl about her feelings and whether she's ready to learn the new toilet training habits.

A child needs to be potty trained just once. Therefore, you have to take that single opportunity and ensure that you are delivering the best methods of teaching on how to be potty trained, to your kid.

You have to make the experience as fun and lively as you can for your child so that it can become an unforgettable adventure for both of you.

Conclusion

Potty training your kid is undoubtedly a stressful yet exciting experience. As your child grows, you need to stay attentive towards their needs and guide them for the way ahead.

Potty training your child is one such phase wherein your child learns to be independent and take care of their body needs. It is important that you potty train your kid on the right time. You do it too soon, and your kid will find it hard to understand and catch the instructions.

You do it too late and your kid will find it difficult to adjust with the changed circumstances which might also lead to low self-esteem.

It is highly recommended to take things slow and be patient throughout the process. Your child might find it tough to get familiar with the training instructions. In such an event, you should not punish or scold your child but rather make them understand the importance of potty training softly and lightly.

We hope this book would have helped you in the entire process and would have assisted you in training your kid. If you liked this book, don't forget to share this book with your friends and family. Also, don't forget to write a review for us on Amazon.

www.ingramcontent.com/pod-product-compliance
Lightning Source LLC
Chambersburg PA
CBHW051719050726

47598CB00003B/968